Miracles Become Monsters

Also by Dominic Kirwan and published by Ginninderra Press

Where Words Go When They Die
Put a Smile On That Face

Dominic Kirwan

Miracles Become Monsters

A gargantuan thank you to my two favourite poets: Leonie Hagstrom and Peter Gate. You are two of the most original writers I have ever had the pleasure to call friends. The boundless creativity and beautiful fearlessness of both of you, and the very original approaches you have to your poetry leave me gobsmacked and inspired every time we meet up.

A special thank you to my friends Andrew Coote and Sally Harbison. You both read every line I write. Your honest feedback is tempered with kindness, vigorous intelligence and heart. You help me to be a better writer.

Thank you to my wonderful sister Bridget Kirwan for her tireless creative assistance with the cover.

Miracles Become Monsters
ISBN 978 1 76041 620 1
Copyright © text Dominic Kirwan 2018
Cover painting: *Zipper De Do Da*, an original work by Dominic Kirwan

First published 2018 by
GINNINDERRA PRESS
PO Box 3461 Port Adelaide SA 5015
www.ginninderrapress.com.au

Contents

Miracles   9

   Steps   11
   When I Still Remembered How To Breathe   16
   Life Fan   22
   Is That a Poem in My Pants…   24
   The Stench of Heaven   26
   F.T.W.   28
   Blush   30
   Actor (For Michae)   33
   My Toilet Is Out To Get Me   35
   Miracle   40
   Pretty Ugly   41
   Pale   42
   The Most Interesting Thing in the Room   44
   (A)Mused   47
   Sloppy Bob   48
   The Second Coming   51
   S.C.R.A.B.B.L.E.D.   52
   Naked Launch   57
   You Wouldn't Read About It   63
   Dream Zero   66
   Something Beautiful   68
   Weeds   70

Monsters   71

   The Giant and the Boy 1   73
   The Peculiar Hum of True Evil   75
   G   78
   Mouse   80
   The First Australian Pope   82

If Only	86
Caught Jester	89
Pork Crackling is the Devil	91
Dark Matters	93
Gimcrack	95
The Giant and the Boy 2	98
A Public Display of Infection	100
Waiting in the Endless Queue for the Afterlife	102
End of Level Boss	105
When He Wrote About the Events That Led To This	108
The Boxer	110
The Words Have Turned Their Backs On Us	112
Unborn Again	114
Balmy Rubble	117
Jesus: A Version	118
The Giant and the Boy 3	121

So lock up your daughter
Lock up your wife
Lock up your back door
And run for your life

TNT – Bon Scott (1946–1980)

I've got your picture, I've got your picture
I'd like a million of them all round my cell
I want a doctor to take your picture
So I can look at you from inside as well

No sex, no drugs, no wine, no women
No fun, no sin, no you
No wonder it's dark

The Vapors (1980)

Miracles

Steps

The First Step
Is to admit that you don't have a problem
Everyone else does

The Second Step
Is to wash your hands of everyone you love
And send them to the gallows

The Third Step
Is to steal a Maserati
And get the fuck out of town
It doesn't matter where you're going
Just drive

The Fourth Step
Is to hold up a bank
And then burn all their money
The system is corrupted
And you're here to save the day

The Fifth Step
Is to break into a brothel
And free the natives
Release them back into the wild
Where they belong

The Sixth Step
Is to attend confession
Admit to the first five steps
And then strangle the priest

With your favourite set of rosary beads
Choke him like a Catholic cock
Caught crowing
Snuff out the light at the end of his tunnel
For promising you
Unattainable redemption

The Seventh Step
Is to drink yourself under the table
And stay there
Just so you'll have somewhere nice to sleep
In the morning
When they close up the bar

The Eighth Step
Is to deliberately lose at poker
And give a naïve gambler
Some schmuck who has never won before
The keys to your stolen car

The Ninth Step
Is to bind and gag a bookstore clerk
And steal all of their Bibles
You'll need them to get into Heaven
When everything goes wrong

The Tenth Step
Is to look yourself in the eye
And try to recognise the stranger
Threaten your reflection with violence
If you have to
Call the police
Report your doppelganger
Identity theft is a serious crime
And you can always deal
With the malfunctioning mirror
Later

The Eleventh Step
Is to break up with yourself
Admit it
The relationship was going nowhere
You should at least agree
To see other people
And then tightly close your eyes

The Twelfth Step
Is to hide

If you're reported missing
People will come looking for you eventually
It's a sign of how much they care
Make sure it's somewhere dark but obvious
You don't want to die of neglect
In the spotlight
With a bottle in your hand

You want to be lost
But eventually found
You want to be loved
By everyone who doesn't matter

The Next Step
Is to revisit the First Step
And start again from there

If you can't be bothered
With the Program
Pour yourself another drink
Because it truly doesn't matter
Step thirteen is a bullshit scene
Step four-hundred-and-eighteen
Is not much better

So turn the music up
Multiply your sex appeal
By absolute zero
Turn the ghost town librarian
That surly lass who stole your heart
When you painted her read
Completely upside down

At the end of it all
When you are totally out of options
Remember to leave your suicide note
Somewhere sexy
Somewhere dark, moist and memorable
Like in the cistern of a leaking toilet
Or in the empty rental space behind your eyes
And write it like you mean it…

Punch the keys
Like they are the faces
Of your fallen gods and nemeses
Of your heroes and your zeros
This is the Final Step
Fuck the pain away

When I Still Remembered How To Breathe

At my funeral,
You're sitting right at the back,
Near the doors
I'm there too, my physical body,
In an open coffin in front of the altar
Pale and cold, dressed more dapper
Than I ever did when I was alive.

The other me, the real me,
The one taking it all in,
He's sitting right next to you
So close I worry that you can still smell me
I haven't showered since I died.

I eye off the nearest exit
Just in case my nicotine starved spectre
Needs to feign smoking
A metaphysical cigarette
Or if I need to escape the waves of pathos
Rippling through these restless,
Yawning pews.

A thought occurs to me,
Ghosts can still suffer from claustrophobia
Relentless social anxiety can still be a thing,
Even when you're dead
Even if you literally can walk right through walls
I guess I could leave here any time I want
Go anywhere I please,

Unwanted, unfelt and unseen
But for now,
I can't bring myself to leave you.

I am curious, I watch you there,
Sitting with your hands buried deep in your lap
It's like your clenched fist is a hand grenade,
And you're attempting to silence it,
To muffle an inappropriate explosion
That would ruin everything.

Stony-cold you are,
The whole time worrying what you will say to people
If they show emotion and in turn expect it from you
Public mourning is not in your social performance arsenal
An empathy overdose would make for a fitting alibi.

You're panicking on the inside,
You need a drink,
I can relate, so do I…
Yet I suspect any attempt I make
At draining a glass of earthly whisky
Would make for a God-awful mess
No, ghosts leave their drinking days behind
Death is the surest cure
For an alcoholic reprobate.

I watch your pupils expand and contract,
Eyelids blinking as if irritated by non-existent fruit flies,
And the inevitability of my recent passing
You are unmoved by the sentiment expected of oneself,
Equally maddened and saddened
By the turn of events that led you here.

I try to touch you, to hold your hand,
To say something stupid in the hopes that you will laugh
But the real me, the guy sitting next to you,
He's out of tangible options
Any attempt to communicate with you is now mired in futility.

Such is the afterlife.

Sure, there are a few tears.
There are the sad, drained faces of my earthly mates,
They just want to make a show of handling things,
Showing respect, dealing with a public forum
That is harder to survive for some than others.
My misty-eyed pall bearer pals
My magnificent sisters and brothers
I slap my transparent knee and laugh,
Wondering if carrying my bloated whale carcass
From the hearse to the church
Has done their backs in
Even here in the afterlife,
I can still be a total bastard.

I look back to you,
So beautifully serene and calm on the surface
Yet inside you are angry
I should know why,
But I can't understand it
Or do I?

Your lip quivers and I wonder if you will cry
I'd still find you impossible, improbable
Sitting there as the hymns drawl on,
Like the sadistic caterwauls
Of an operatic catholic peacock,
Doped to the colourful, feathery eyeballs
By the mystery of Jesus and his magical blood.

The congregated few attempt to sing in unison
But it is fruitless
One person, I suspect a middle-aged woman,
She is singing over the top of all the other voices
A midlife crisis diva with delusions of grandeur
Most probably
Varicose vain with thick matronly ankles
Hovering above the tone deaf miscreants
Filling this chapel of temporary grief
With musical banality.

She is in-key and she knows it.
She belts out the chorus –
'Lamb of god, you take away the sinnnnsss of the woooorrrrrld!'
As if God is more impressed by good singing
Than anything else
I look around but I can't locate her
But I can see her in my head
Odd, you'd think she would have
Straddled the organ player by now
Pouting like Madonna,
(The popular culture version of course)
She's singing her way to heaven
And making everyone else look bad
I guess that's the point for some people.

Jesus is watching me
He is watching me, watching you,
Watching the insides of your rib cage
I count each of your heartbeats
As if it were evidence of how much you care
Do you care?
I can barely tell
Is this an inconvenience?

The cross above the altar looms ominously
An unhappy man all scantily clad and wood carved,
Peering at me through two bleeding slits
Like I've done something wrong
Like I deserve to be here
Like I am beyond redemption
Yes, that's right, Jesus.

All that I am and all that I was is…wrong
There is no changing this.

Caucasian Jehovah,
Such a smug motherfucker
He's all driven nails,
Crown of thorns and deflated, defeated eyes
'What the fuck are you looking at?'
I stand up and angrily shout,
With more diminished purpose than I intended
But no sound comes out of my mouth
It's about then that I realise I can't even see myself,
Let alone castigate the guy who looks
Like he's been tortured and bullied into oblivion.

I really should apologise to Jesus
But I suspect he gets that a lot
It's probably overkill
I decide to forgive him
For being such a judgemental bastard,
For being in extreme pain,
Put on display like a martyred monkey
In a Cathaholic petting zoo.

I go to sit back down next to you
Yet you are gone.
You fled the scene just in time too,
Slipped out of the Church
While my mind was wandering elsewhere
Left me for dead,
Just like I left you
Once upon a time,
When I still remembered how to breathe.

Life Fan

The most rebellious thing you can do is love life
Despite the sickness lapping at your eyelids
Despite the fear keeping you locked away
Despite the fact you know it's all coming down
The amoral rapture
The poisoned slice of birthday cake
That you bite into anyway
Knowing Death is not sweeter
Knowing Death will be far briefer
Knowing Death will be an unavoidable cliché
Knowing you don't want it all to end
Not just yet
Not with all this beautiful mayhem
To describe
To embrace
To run from as you leap across the canyon
That exists to keep you from knowing anything for certain
That keeps you from knowing life
That keeps you drooling on yourself
Dribbling like a bed wetting passenger
On your way to something better

Love yourself anyway

Love yourself as you feel your face growing paler
Love yourself as the sun sets behind your back
Love yourself as the pills steal your insanity
Love yourself as the world grows numb
Love yourself as you sit alone in the dark

Love life anyway

Despite the bigotry of strangers
Despite ruination and unkind fictions
Despite the past and how it defines you
Despite all the beautiful delusions that bind you
Despite the fact that you have not
And simply cannot
Change

Smile like it matters
Laugh like you've already won
Kiss like you're kissable
Bleed all over the memory of when it all went wrong
Then throw it all away

Say it: 'Life is fucking wonderful.'

So there.

Is That a Poem in My Pants or Do You Just Want To Read Me?

There are red stop lights
In her eyes
A green glow
In my heart

I just need to drink more
This is step thirteen
AA is just a wasted God away
I just need to hide
Some place haunted
Let the ghosts come looking for me

Yes, hide and write
Let my words do the seducing
Keep a pen in my pants
Yes, rot and write
Let my fiction create friction
Keep a poem in my pants
Something romantic and horrifying
For the ladies…
Rolling their eyes on the inside
As I jest, unimpressed
As I drink and smoke and choke
On wonderment
On the poetry
Swirling in their pretty purple eyes

Everything about me is in reverse

I feel petrified and exposed and fragile and frightened and
　　ugly and deformed and…

Easily painted by my own deficiencies
Into a bloated corner
Where Necro Nonsensical is my name

Kiss me
Cover me in fragrant dirt
Kiss me
Gently and without malice
Kiss me
Anywhere
In the garden or the gutter
In the sky amongst the snarling stars
Kiss me
In moments such as these
When I feel so weak with desire
That I forget my own name
I forget my lines
I lose my place in the kissing-booth queue
Thinking of such kissing
Drowning on an ocean bed of you

Still…

It's not a circus mirror
It just looks at me that way

The Stench of Heaven

There is nothing left for us
Miracles become monsters
That's just the way it goes
We knew better when we were first born
Covered in blood and
Breathing in the perfumed plume
Of hospital bleach
Squinting blindly
Not even knowing our own names

Now we march in formation
Now we feign imagination

Now we stall before we've started
Now we pray to ourselves for forgiveness
Now the mirror molests our features
Now the scales call us names
Now we rewind our clocks
Now we look forward to yesterday

There is nothing left of you
I knelt in your menstrual blood
And muttered hallelujahs
While you sweetly whispered my name
I snorted the last of your ashes
Like cheap cut cocaine
I swam between your ears
And ran like foul nectar through your hair
Begging you to stay the same

Now the stench of heaven calls me
Like a rodent
Praying for a red-light pussy
To enfold me
Like a statue
Praying to Michelangelo
To resculpt me

Your train of thoughts is in reverse
The tracks in your arms are deepening
The crack in your smile is spreading
The mind shaft is collapsing
Dirt and debris, raining down
Like holy fire upon you
For the world we knew is gone

F.T.W.

I wanna fuck the world and be loved for it
I wanna bury you while you're still smiling
I wanna drug you with sugar pills and play Placebo
I wanna tear off your face and wear it to church
I wanna dress up in yellow Spandex and fight Wolverine
I wanna do tequila shots at AA meetings and refuse to share

I wanna jelly wrestle nuns and break the habit
I wanna sucker punch Gandhi and steal his lunch money
I wanna bully the bullies and drink their tears
I wanna read the Bible and jerk off to Revelations
I wanna save up and buy the bank
I wanna roll up my sleeves and do nothing
I wanna have sex in corpse paint and funeral ash
I wanna fuck in a freshly dug grave
I wanna lather myself in second-hand lube and cardamom seeds
I wanna play naked Twister with a grizzly bear
I wanna dance like people are watching
I wanna spank Jesus
I wanna lecture him about forgiveness
I wanna drink the holy water with tequila and a slice of lime
I wanna write poems about you that don't fucking rhyme

I wanna leap out of a birthday cake
I wanna do death metal karaoke
I wanna shove a flash drive up my arse and shit Gigabytes
I wanna photograph the photographer
I wanna film the film beyond the camera
I wanna sign fake tits with animal tested lipstick like I'm famous
I wanna crap in the fruit and vegetable section
I wanna take a sly dump in the all-you-can-eat buffet
I wanna vomit down Santa's chimney and dampen the fire
I wanna scare the elves into leaving
I wanna eat tuna-safe dolphin from a rusty tin

I wanna sink my teeth into your op shop heart
I wanna fall in love with shadows
I wanna weep bad poetry and dream of clever meat
I wanna break back into the asylum

Blush

In the year 2046, after the Fifth Great War,
Humanity was all but ready to implode
Devouring itself from the inside
Drunk on the fumes of its own wretched vanity.

The Aliens,
Being somewhat careful about their timing,
Had arrived just in time.

The effects of the virus had been relentless,
Imbuing people with strange physical deformities.
People's noses and genitals, confused by the virus,
Had decided to relocate.
They gradually shifted from their correct anatomical position,
Roaming across their owner's skin like psychotic slugs.
They set up camp somewhere else,
Somewhere that seemed safe,
But was usually entirely inappropriate,
Like on the back of the knee or on the side of the face.

It was not uncommon to wake
And find that an eye was missing,
Only to discover it on the inner thigh
Or at the base of the spine.

People's perspectives soon began to change.

In some ways, the massive hunt
And subsequent culling
Of the world's mirrors that followed
Was understandable.
Now everyone was ugly.
It didn't matter if you were a movie star,
A street urchin, a catwalk model or a janitor.
The fact was that your nipples
Had traded places with your ears,
And there was nothing you could really do about it.

For the Aliens, it was all too easy.
They brought with them giant reflective orbs.
Distorting the humans further,
Showing them how impossibly hideous they had become.

The Aliens decided to use the media for their gain,
Just as the humans had done before.
They lured people from their homes
With television specials about the New Hollywood.
They broadcast glitzy advertisements
For the Neverland Plastic Surgery Clinic.
Promising painless genital relocation operations
And a quick and easy way
To displace that embarrassing sphincter
That had set up shop on one's chin.

Physical change was going cheap,
The ads guaranteed,
For three, monthly instalments
Of sixty thousand nine hundred and ninety-nine dollars,
Those with scarred blue skin
Could be pink all over again.

Humanity became a circus sideshow.
People were locked away in overcrowded invisible cages,
With nothing but genetically modified bananas,
Vanity Fear catalogues
And elaborate make-up kits to play with.

The Aliens watched closely,
Enthralled with the antics of their new pets.
Millions of deformed monkeys
Writhed in captive futility,
Striving to cover up the unwanted testicle
Growing from their third cheek
With cheap Alien blush.

Actor (For Michae)

I am an actor and I love you.

Those are my lines I didn't write them
I just read them to you out loud
from behind a broken camera lens
that beckons me, expecting me to perform.

I am an actor and I don't understand
this play that I am in.
I am an actor and absolutely everything
I say is a performance.

In the dressing room I practise
saying romantic lines to myself
but instead, in the ethereal mirror,
I only see YOUR face.

I am an actor
and if I am feeling insecure
I just text my performance in.

My award winning roles
are all based on past life dancing,
and the statues passed to me on plasticine podiums
are plastic simulacra of golden gods
that no one worships any more.

Still, the movie studios are ecstatic,
the fans are dying from the pandemic.

I long to kiss your social media profile
but my tongue is glued to the screen.

You have sewn me in,
you have captured my words
and you persist
in embroidering them to my chest.

You are miles away,
yet still we somehow hold hands
on a bacterial beach
scattered with marooned, weeping whales.
We are not strong enough to push them back into the ocean.
They will die of neglect and eventually so will we.

We are only dreaming all of this, my dear,
our real lives are far more than we can bear.

The whales are screaming…
they are deathly still and they are barely breathing.
We cannot save them any more than we can save ourselves.

Still, I am an actor and I love you…

My Toilet Is Out To Get Me

My Toilet is out to get me
Revenge
For shitting on him
For way too long
I suspect that's where all the missing socks have gone
He ate them
He ate my flash drives
He swallowed all the pens
Every cigarette lighter I buy goes the way of hungry porcelain
Hair ties, keys, hell, even my smile is gone
Devoured by the gaping jaws of my loo

My Toilet is mobile
Every time I leave the flat
Legs mechanically sprout from his sides
He disconnects from the sewage chute on the wall
And roams freely, trudging from room to room
He rummages through my cupboards
Searching for ways to further sabotage my life

My Toilet hunts for loose change
And important paperwork
My electricity got disconnected
When I failed to pay the bill
I cursed at him in the darkness
Of our shared bathroom
Washing my hands for the hundredth time
It's an imperative, repetitive ritual
And if you don't use toilet paper
You simply have to

My Toilet logs on to my Facebook account
When I am absent
He unfriends my entire family
Insults my digital friends
He writes disgusting poems and posts them online
As if he's really me

My Toilet surfs the web for expensive, over-sized dildos
And pays for them with my debit card
There's far too many to count now
And I'm too self-conscious to throw them out
The garbage collector already thinks I'm a freak
I attempt to flush them away
But they keep popping up
In the most inconvenient places

My Toilet eats all my underwear
If only he would regurgitate a few pairs
Like he does with the dildos
Cos I don't feel safe going commando
And needing to constantly replace them
In both Target, Woolies and Lingerie for Ladies
Is beginning to arouse suspicion
The skinny blue-haired checkout chick
With the septum piercing and the hip lisp
Who is always at the register
Every fucking register no matter where I go
She's starting to look at me funny

Perhaps she knows something is up?
Maybe I should ask her out on a date?
We could go back to my place afterwards
She could get to know my Toilet
Surely then she'd understand

My Toilet eats all my food
He cooks in the kitchen for hours
Somehow everything he conjures up
Turns out gourmet and delicious
I've tasted the leftovers
Of his chicken parmigiana
And it was absolutely to die for

I suspect my Toilet watches cooking shows
There is no other explanation for his talent
Masterchef is a master class
In culinary perfection
Apparently everyone who watches it
Turns out a far better cook
My Toilet is no exception
If he went on that show
He'd most likely make it to the final ten

My Toilet is out to get me
Although I can't be absolutely certain
Maybe it's all in my head?
Like the time he ate the neighbour's cat

Fuzzy Muff wandered inside my flat
Stretched, clawed at the couch
Cast her judgemental gaze over the mess
Snubbed her Russian Blue nose in my general direction
And proceeded to eat the sirloin strips
On the kitchen bench
Left there, I suspect
To marinate in a ceramic bowl
By my talented, culinary lavatory

She ate the bloody lot too
Right in front of me
As if to flaunt her feline superiority

Thinking she might be thirsty
After such a hearty meal
I ushered her into the bathroom
And closed the door behind her

There was quite a commotion
Much gurgling and hissing and screeching
Followed finally by a distinct poetic burp

No one has seen Fuzzy Muff in ages
Her upset owners questioned me at great length
I am not responsible for the actions
Of my rogue lavatory
But at the same time,
I'm no tattletale
No scurrilous rat
So I didn't say a thing

My Toilet can't be trusted
Trust me
I know him well
Yet sometimes I do wonder
As I absently stir Mongolian beef
With a twelve-inch black dildo
And as I stare, misty-eyed
At yet another goddamn cooking show
I simply cannot imagine
What shit would be like without him
Like a flushed familiar
Caught in a foggy bathroom mirror
He is my only friend

Miracle

Spitting in the face of the Gift
Life, blood, breath, improbable
I am a grain of sand
In an indestructible molecule
What more can I know than this?

I can feel the unrelenting tide
Circling my throat
Like a lusty shark
I can hear the ocean
Whispering, an old salty ghost
Haunting my insolence

I love
And I am loved
How dare I question this
How dare I long for more than THIS

The kiss
A single sperm, clamping its maws
Into an ovary of pearl
Missed, like this miracle
Camouflaged by conceit, the Gift
Of always

And I will return to oblivion…

Pretty Ugly

What would it be like if they truly knew you?
Would you get up off the ground?
Would you dust yourself off and look them in the eye?
Would you cry?
Would you empty your pockets of uncut diamonds?
Would you rain down bones upon your enemies?
Would you rattle your shackles till they fell away?
Would you shuffle off into the night?
Would you say goodbye…?

lie with me
one last time
under this defiant sky
freckled with dead stars

What would it be like to leave it all behind?
Would you wade through the literary mud?
Would you succeed when all you've ever done is fail?
Would you bail?
Would you strip the tree of apples and flee the garden naked?
Would you forgive the god that abandoned you?
Would you drink from the fountain of youth and tear out your eyes?
Would you smash the very last mirror?
Would it make you feel better?
Would you say goodbye…?

lie with me
one last time
beneath this raging black hole
devouring all

Our hearts are not safe
They never were

Pale

Drill a hole in me
Fill me with alley trash crack
And pink concrete
Then seal me up
Got a straightjacket smile
Miming the words
Of madly muttering strangers
Walking in circles
On regretful street corners

That insignificant little voice
Singing like a caged bird
Deep inside my tar-pit head
Once a murmur
It has become a murderer
And these derangements
They have opened a door
I cannot close

All my words are pale
All my wrongs are pale
Love is steadily ascending

I can feel the tears
Gathering behind my eyes
They wait there
Like enemies of the cold
Like an infinitum of unattended funerals
Like the sweet taste of compassion and sex
Like the unhinged laughter
Of a trillion romantic lunatics
Chasing one invisible heart

Bleeding to feel
Something
Anything
Everything
Aching to love and love and love
And die for it
Kill for it
Even if I don't have to

I have no more time for cages
I am nothing but demon pieces
Death show passion
And mercurial light

The Most Interesting Thing in the Room

You know things are messed up
When the television
Is the most interesting thing in the room
There can be ten of us
Or just one
And still all eyes will be on that screen

Advertisements
Sitcoms
The news
The weather
Soap operas
Crime dramas
Documentaries
Movies
Hollywood snot
Platinum popcorn
All of it is more fascinating
Than any single human being

Our own channels never change that much
And there is rarely anything about us
Worth watching
We are comfortable
To let the television to do the entertaining
We laugh at its jokes
We groan at its mediocrity
Yet every now and then
It says something profound
And our lives feel more liveable
And we feel less alone

Television cares about us
It moonlights
As a mirror
And we feel ugly, beautiful
Insignificant and important
All at once
And we look to it for guidance
It knows a lot more about the world
Than we do

Somewhere behind the screen
There is a glowing, flickering
Hyper-reality
An essence we could cling to
Yet it is always just out of reach

Maybe we're just scared of each other
Maybe we don't want to be stared at
Laughed at
Mocked
Congratulated
We'd rather watch someone else
Win the fucking game show

How do all of those people fit inside that screen?
So thin
So flat
Like the world used to be
Perhaps we aren't like that?
Maybe if we could join them
We would matter more?

Some of us would do anything
To matter

Maybe we purchased a television
So that the world would make sense
Truth is
It rarely does
Not really
Do we?

I am happy for the television
It always knows what to say
It lies to us
And nobody really minds
It is popular
It is cruel
And still nobody cares
We forgive the television
For tricking us
Into submission
Truth is, the television is full of shit
And the annihilation of our consciousness
Is merely a side effect
Of our love affair
With the television

I don't want to change the channel any more
I wanna put an axe right through the screen
And then smile…
Like I did something worth celebrating
Like it actually fucking matters.

(A)Mused

She is an impossible poem
The one that I could not write
Singularly scarred
With pretty wounds that feast on unbelievers
Camped within her weeping borders
She shrinks and kinks and thinks
Of don't-dream-it's-over Police
And morning terror alabaster

She rules her kingdom
With tempestuous mirrors
The Omega Maiden of rogue riddles
Just bypassing the height line
For an imaginary roller coaster ride
Through a Shangri-La bazaar

I cannot write her
She is already written
(A)Mused and past life disabused
Of my shady notions

I cannot read her
This ancient tome with no cover
Just depths that defy design

Sloppy Bob

1.

I left her and she was liberated.
I left her and the transition decapitated my sense of self.
Boo-who et cetera.

Now my severed, self-pitying head,
It rolls just a few metres in front of me wherever I go
I take my metaphorical, decapitated ego on leisurely strolls
Through abandoned theme parks
And red-light district cemeteries
I have it on a tight leash
I call it Sloppy Bob

Keeping a pet is good for the soul, so they say
I just follow the trail of blood, ooze and watermelon pips
That lay in the aftermath of Sloppy Bob's wavering, slobbery gait
Such is the crushed, obliterated fruit
Of this burning cannery that I call recovery

Who needs emotional GPS
When I have Sloppy Bob to lead the way?

Love is all about the disco
Mirror balls are the meatball gravy gallstones
Of the astral plane
Rescued from one's arse like an unpolishable turd
That has been rolled in glitter

Love is all about the 70s
It's like having a feverish Saturday night that never ends
Your bell bottoms swirl
Your flared pants ride up a little too high in the crotch
Sequins and that seventies chest hair returns
It burns
Yet you just keep on dancing

Perhaps I am a reverse narcissist?
Maybe I beheld my reflection
In the water's rippling surface and thought -
How utterly horrendous, what an abomination…
But…hmmmmm…how very interesting.

Haemorrhoids guffaw
Flowers bloom and then devour unsuspecting bees
The impossibility of love
The failure of that doomed union
It is infinite
It is everywhere I look and in everything I perceive

2.

I have taken to staring at the wall
For numb, elongated periods
I drink and I smoke
And I stare at this one particular damn brick
It is exactly the same as all of the other bricks
With the exception that it is directly below the light switch

It is a special brick

I have not named it, this brick, nor will I
Nothing clever comes to mind
I live within the delusion that one day
It will suddenly slide out of the wall and fall to the ground
In a puff of cement fairy dust
And it will reveal the answer to everything

In truth, I suspect this will never happen
But maybe, just maybe,
I will lock eyes with someone
Through that hole on the other side of the wall
A beautiful stranger
Who embodies everything I yearn for…
We will fall in love clumsily
Like in a trashy but charming TV movie
Based on a book that doesn't yet exist

And then she will ask for her brick back

The Second Coming

The deposit
The gambler
The casino is a sperm bank
And the Devil is a big spender
But Jesus…he saves
So have some faith
Because a rainy day
Is on its way

S.C.R.A.B.B.L.E.D.

I was just minding my own Guinness
Performing a poorly timed comedy routine
Punch pun drunk
For the empty auditorium
Stretching out in every direction
Infinitely within my mind
When I noticed something
For the first time
Someone was sitting in the back
An audience of one
They weren't laughing
But still, they bothered to show up
And that's what counts

Had they brought a ticket?
Would I get a slice of THAT pie?
I adjusted my testicles
Reached for my binoculars
Became overly excited and promptly fainted

When I awoke I was in my own bed
Someone was knocking at the door
I pretended I was asleep
I feigned dreaming
Still
Knock, knock, knock…

Grumbling, I staggered to the door
I opened it
A man wearing moccasins and a tweed suit
Smiled a toothy, facile grin
His eyes were raisins
Buried deep
His cheeks were acne scarred
He may or may not
Have been hiding an erection
It was still too early to tell
Then again, perhaps he wasn't a Mormon
And I had nothing to fear

Without a Word
He unleashed a tattered Scrabble set
From beneath his arm
Presenting it like a box of chocolates
To an unknowing valentine
He said, 'You are playing with Death.'

I couldn't argue with that
Besides, I quite liked Scrabble
So I ushered him into my chambers
Put on a brew of coffee
And proceeded to scramble some unfertilised eggs

What is your name? I asked
He merely winked knowingly
And began to set up the board

I reached for a dictionary
And proceeded to tear out
The more obvious pages
I shredded them with fervour
I threw the remains into the air above us
The paper fragments rained down
Like unique little snowflakes
Like unique little people
Wafting on ghostly air currents
The room cooled
I shivered on the inside
Built a snowman out of my thoughts

We sipped coffee from bone thimbles
I burnt the fucking eggs
He ate them any way
It was very nice of him

We began to play the Game

After a few hours of sweaty, literary mayhem
And a plethora of medium-scoring constructions
Like ABYSS
On a double word score
And GREASE
But not the movie, so it was allowed
I began to suspect he was going easy on me
Why?

Every triple word score
Was a tempting prospect
A fertile hole, unmined
Every Z or Q or X
It soon became obvious
Was in HIS possession
Yet they remained unused
Every red square
On the edges of the board
Like a neat box containing Marx
Remained unpopulated by the Word

I looked at the letters before me on the table
I had an uninterrupted line of four Us
And an O and a P
It was all over
I needed LENT
But there was no such word
Upon the board

I lost badly
But he was nice about it
Real nice like
A gentleman and one hell of a player
I shook his hand firmly
He embraced me, suddenly
And I felt his erection press into my side
I don't always like being right
But there it was
An unapologetic boner

I ushered him out
Winning excites people in strange ways, I thought
I shut the door behind him
Collapsed onto my mattress
And went about feigning still more dreams
And snoring

When I awoke I was a new man
Despite temptation
I gave up Scrabble for 40 days
I never played with Death again.

Naked Launch

Countdown… 10–9–8…

We dissect life
As if it were a quantifiable entity
I don't trust my own eyes, ears and
my know, it knows very little
I suspect
That everything that comes out of my mouth
Is a regurgitation of something broken
That was designed to stay that way

My candle burns to the left
I just can't be fucked buying the T-shirt

7–6…

The Titanic did the undrinkable
The drowning life saver
Tasted so sweet
She seemed unsinkable

Oil wrestling became popular
With the poltergeists of bikini barons
Reclining in luxury on deckchairs
Trying for the perfect ego tan
In the afterlife
On abandoned oil tankers

Now barrels of laughter are going so cheap
We cannot help but pollute
The pale, ill oceans
Raging in our hearts
With non-biodegradable mirth

Suicide has become an advertisement
For displaced
Product placement protests
Jesus approves
But he would, wouldn't he?
If we ever did have a clue
We still missed the point
Entirely

5–4…

People watch
Bored, rolling their eyes
As a guy rises from the gutter
He tears bacon strips
From Western Capitalist Pigs
And eagerly eats them

We listen
As they attempt to squeal along
To the disinformation,
Masturbatory national anthem
In unison
Completely in and out
Of auto-tune

God sweating dollar signs
Are wept from crying
Red, white and blue eyes
And we all love to get high, Maaaannnnn…
On the fumes
Of someone else's burning flag:
Church,
Mosque,
Synagogue,
Temple,
Jail cell.
Hell…
Of someone else's idea
Of what it means to be human
et cetera
et cetera
et cetera.

World War Three
Has become Weird War Four,
Wank War Five,
Six and 7-Eleven
Are cumming soon
To a cineplex near you

So purchase your tickets early
Bring a box of tissues
And some moisturising cream
Just in case
This shit has got so fucking crazy
We have lost count completely
Without knowing who to kill
We wage war upon ourselves

Terror is an abstract notion
The war on love
Has been reduced to a photograph
Of two university sweethearts
In a year book
Burnt to cinders in a drunken fit
At a beach party bonfire

The night after that
One of them blew their brains out
With a gun
The other one got over it
A little too quickly

Nobody can tell you why

3–2…

The mist clears
The waters magically part
Like the legs of an exquisite whore
Moaning molten gold

We find ourselves naked and exposed
Viewed by a reality television sky
Hovering infinitely above us
As we cuss, preen and dread
Lying on our backs
On foaming mattress flower beds

Chaos butterflies and honey drizzling bees
Flutter in formation
Kissing our eyelids and tickling our lips
And sweetly, softly
They beckon us to speak

Still, we say nothing that is heard
Still, by saying everything
We say nothing at all

Yet as the Zeitgeist passes through us
Something strange and thrilling
Shimmers in the shadows
And it begins to take on a life of its own

Suddenly
For a brief, fleeting moment
Our silence becomes a roar that could deafen the Gods
The abyss finally smiles back
It knows us
It understands us
It forgives us

But is it too late?
Perhaps we should return
To our asbestos-lined coffins
And wait…

Perhaps we are dreaming all of this
For the very last time

Then again
Perhaps it is now…or forever
And this is merely the beginning
Of a most beautiful lie

1.

Blast off?

You Wouldn't Read About It

I could not seem to write anything
Worth reading
I tried everything
I chained myself to a keyboard
But much too soon
I wriggled free
I built several different-sized cages
Meant to fit
In Matryoshka doll stages
I got inside the smallest
And waited
For the words to come to me
I was rewarded with the clanging of iron
The jangling of skeleton keys

My pages bristled in anger
Empty, blank and alone
They raged against the cages
They screamed at startled strangers
They blamed me
For I was not even a sweeping desert
My mind a barren sandpit
Filled with tabby cat crap
And half built castles
Remote in their moats
Steadily filling with the water
From a dripping tap nearby

I writhed
Clawing at the edges
Of an ink-filled chasm
The tiny voices in my ears
Chuckled like illiterate critters
Music crackled like a phonograph
Circling an empty dance floor

So I danced
Like a macabre silhouette
And I cried
Like a stale crumb of bread
And the luminescence of nothing
It became my something
And I roared
Like a confused tornado
And tore apart all but the calm
In my eye

For I found a voice
And to all but the gallows
The soon to hang shadows
I remained indecipherable
An echo of displacement
And snoring pride
The glimmer in the eye
Of a snapped needle
The last drip of poison
In an endless ocean

The awkward feeling one gets
As the walls of the labyrinth
Come tumbling down
And you realise
Underneath all that rubble
That you are still writing…

Dream Zero

She is a poisonous sunflower
She is a ray of radioactive sunshine
She is a set of wet lips
Wrapped around a White House cigar

She is premenstrual tension
Your last shot heroine
She deliberately ran you over
At the zebra zoo crossing
With her red eyes glowing
Driving your very own car

She is a stationary drifter
She is the unphotoshopped picture
That she took of herself
While visiting your body at the morgue

She is a feminist who loves men
Who genuinely love women

She is a shooting scar
She is caustic empathy and armpit hair
She is a philosophically stimulating derrière
She is a brightly burning brazier
She is an ambitious op shop connoisseur
An under-discovered star

She is the excitement one gets
When you are counting down sheep
From one thousand to none
When you simply can't sleep
And it's all you can do
Not to think of her

When you are edging ever closer
To that diminishing number
As the last electric black sheep
Leaps over the fenced off area
In your festering heart
And you are just happy
To be in the arms of her ghost
Dreaming of zero

Something Beautiful

If you look hard enough
You can see right through the screen
If you squint your eyes
There are wonders to discover
Your God, your Patron Saint of Suicide
She weeps black and white rainbows
There is something beautiful on the other side

If you believe in me
There is nothing I cannot do
If you take my shaking hands in yours
I will steady the trembling horizon
Smother you in rogue kisses
Like a punch-drunk Lothario
I will fill your lungs with sweet bleach
Wipe away the tar, the cancer and the scars
I will drown your heart in cheap moonshine
I will complete you
I will delete the parts of you that have died
There is something beautiful on the other side

There is so much here to love
Even in the blackout
I can still make out your tearful, glassy eyes
There is so much here to see
Even in the unfathomable darkness
There are reasons to hold onto each other
There is something beautiful on the other side

I am here
I have always been here
Waiting for you
Swooning in cruel moonlight
Craving someone I will never meet
I will wait forever, an eternity
If I have to…

I do not want to face the world alone

Weeds

I came across the mountain with a notion
On the other side
There would be trees worth climbing
Yet weeds are all I see
A rash of dying butterflies
Wings already pinned to the lip
Of a hollow volcano
And they wonder why I'm still smiling
I can see as far as they'll let me

The horizon is a dartboard
I never miss
My glasses help me see the empty ones
I'm blind without drinking a drop
Can't see a damn thing without them
It's quicker that way
It's called the sun and it will melt me

My ghost called
I told him there might be a delay
On the death thing
He got back in the mirror
And I chained him there
He's happy to wait for a while
Against his will

Monsters

The Giant and the Boy 1

The Giant, with his rubbery pockmarked face
and his piercing stare.
He glares into the Boy's eyes,
searching for a reason to punish the Boy.
Looking for signs of guilt.

The Boy doesn't know what he's done wrong.
But he feels guilty.
He always feels guilty when the Giant has been drinking.
When the Giant looks at him
like he knows something the Boy does not.
He is guilty, and the Giant can tell.
It's all over his face.

The Giant's breath is hot and stinks of the drink.
The Boy turns his face away.
The Giant grabs him by the hair
and drags him into the bathroom.
Now standing in front of the mirror,
the Boy doesn't so much as whimper.
He looks at the floor,
anywhere but in the mirror.
He wants to be anywhere but here.
He thinks about running away
and the guilt washes over him,
like the Giant's hot stinky breath.

Wack!

The Giant delivers a blow to the back of the Boy's head

Wack!

The Giant grabs the Boy's hair and wrenches his head back.
He forces the Boy to look at the mirror.

The Giant doesn't have to ask any more.
The Boy knows what is expected of him.
'Maggot,' he says,
Pointing at the smaller of the two figures in the glass.
The Giant nods and ruffles the Boy's hair,
Almost affectionately.
He is suddenly pleased with the Boy.
He grunts and staggers out of the bathroom.

The Boy feels that he has been good.
And he stands like that,
Staring at the Maggot in the mirror,
The little Maggot with tears streaming down his cheeks.

The Peculiar Hum of True Evil

Wandering on the peripheries
I met a blind junkie with beautiful eyes
I gave him a needle and the last of my stash
Stole his poor, neglected mirror
And then I watched him slowly die
Grinning like a fiend of freedom
Who had lost the will to love

Wandering along the edge of the cliff
I met a suicidal Messiah
Sporting a mind-of-its-own erection
I asked him for forgiveness in advance
Tied a pretty yellow bow
Around the source of his confusion
Then gave him one final push
It was the nudge of encouragement he needed
He had promised me
He would redeem my latent psycho-sexuality
Once his body hit the ground

Wandering in Wonderland
I met a wannabe Alice
With murder on her mind
I armed her with a rifle
Yet she was too late, too late
For the unimportant bugger-the-bunny date
Still, I convinced her
That it was open rabbit season

Wandering in Heaven
I held up a 7-Eleven
I seduced the pretty checkout chick
Stuffed my pockets
With minimum wage memories
And obsolete virginity
I tore pages from her diary
I worshipped at the altar of her bones
I filled my rotting soul with candy clones
I promptly fled as my black heart bled
Leaving the lust and love I learnt alone

Wandering on the boundaries
I met a celebrity with a thought disease
I prescribed her placebo medication
And fed her fame pills
I gave her my autograph and posed for pictures
The next morning
She was pregnant with complications
I solemnly swore to a jury of whores
That it simply wasn't me

Wandering in Hell
I met the Devil, he was playful
He whipped out his Monopoly
I set up the burning board
We played and I prayed
Until I lost my mind

Three red-light district hotels
And then Bond Street
I left him there, with everything I once held dear
I stole a Get-Out-of-Jail-Free card
For I knew I would need it later
When he came to collect my soul

Wandering in the time machine
I was ambushed by Margaret Thatcher
She wore a Reunion-Jack Strap-on
She bent me over her Lincoln
As if I was the Falklands War
She called me her sweetest Argentina
But she didn't cry for me
I stunned her with my Ronald Ray-Gun
And staggered away shame free

Wandering in the shadows
I met a prostitute with a heart of gold
She kissed me and then she paid me
When I told her she had it backwards
She kissed me again more deeply
And stole my broken heart away

G

Norman manoeuvred the young woman's head
so that it rested snugly between the steel teeth of the vice.
His pulse raced and he pumped the lever feverishly
until he was certain there was sufficient grip.

He struggled impatiently with her drugged limbs,
arranging them so they didn't impede access
to the freshly shaved patch in the centre of her scalp.

Norman finally folded his arms and took a deep breath.
A wry grin spread across his face like a rash.
He stood back to marvel at his unconscious bride.
He stooped down to retrieve the axe.

'Hold still, Sugar, not long now,' he drooled.

The chloroform could lose its effect at any moment.
Norman knew he must make haste,
lest his lover should suddenly awake.
That would not do at all, not now,
not after all his meticulous planning.

He heaved the axe above his head
and with a dexterous motion
brought it down on the girl's skull,
slicing a trail through her skin
and precious white bone.

The girl's head split open
like an over-ripe melon,
spewing emulsions of neural fibre
and sweet blood.

He wiped a bloody hand across his forehead.
This is thirsty work, he thought.

He proceeded to pry the crack open with both hands
and the lips of the crevice parted further
to accommodate his fingers.
The girl's mandible began to spasm.
Norman drove his hand deep into the cerebral tissue,
crudely severing the lateral hemispheres
with his thumb and forefinger.

'Easy, Baby, it's got to be in here somewhere,' Norman said.

He pierced the temporal lobe with his finger
and found what he was looking for.
The magical jackpot.
His eyes brimmed with tears of joy
as he eagerly massaged the surrounding fluid
into the mysterious lump.
Careful not to overwhelm by pressing too hard
or too directly into the mysterious spot.

'Oooohhh, Sweety, you found it, finally you found it,'
the girl, half conscious, began to moan.

'I love you, Cupcake,' said Norman.

'Ooohhh, I love you too, Sugar Plum,' she groaned.

And the blood descended
Like sweet nectar,
To well in her pretty blue eyes.

Mouse

Send me your miracles and your monsters
Send me your plucked out eyes and
The pungent perfume of your spent loins
Hold me in the jaws of your slavering mouse

Oh, how you ache to delete me
An abortable foetus
With the sniffles, a cold, the flu,
A dreamlike, pustular virus
I am infinitely disposable
I am just a sick click away
I am yours

These icons
They line up like neon cockroaches
Twitching, glowering ravenously
All along the edges
Of the unearthly garden of Gethsemane

Drag me across your raging database ocean
Dangle me over the recycle bin
Waiting like garbage, like Godot
In the corner of your mind

Live bait for the monster
A fang-toothed rat, snickering
A fattened cock, no longer crowing
Just muffled flat screen screams
A slit throat and shattered beak
No longer pecking
A plump sacrifice
For the rotund belly of your mad god

My blood
Pixellated and photoshopped
Into perfect imperfection
Trickling into the digital abyss
That exists below

Your only purpose is to uncreate
Your only rationale
Is to delete, delete, delete then repeat
To deprogram
My dancing monkey hologram
Soon hit by a fuck truck
Hard driving
Along the one-way information superhighway

So send me your miracles and your monsters
Save your tears
And I will back up mine
Slacken the vice-like maw of your mouse
And then let me go…

The First Australian Pope

He masturbates three times a day
He is an explosives expert
The mirror is a dartboard
For a rampant pimple outbreak
It seems will never end

At school he basks in the glory
Of every perverted story
Retelling details
Of toxic lubricants
Better left unsaid
They're his friends
They listen and squirm
He's honest to a fault
Just so they might laugh
At things they themselves
Would never say

Yet on the inside
He is falling
He is always falling

Guilty giggling in the schoolyard
The soundtrack
To a psychotic puberty
To a violent God
That lashes back
That attacks
Every time he prays
That the Beast inside him
Might go away

Every mark
Scrawled on the wall
Is a secret triumph
A hidden score
Wiping away the filth
Denying eyes crying
Teeth gnashing
Soul thrashing
The savage bite of God's whip
A symptom of hell fire
One more mark
Then another
Another night
Without God hating his guts
Pleasing the Master
Hands above the covers
God reinstating the Priest
His Mother swears is there

Bright lights in his future
The Saints are calling
This God is calling
Always they are calling him

He swells with guilt
Like a confused teenage cock
Crowing into the void

Mother
Snooping for smutty magazines
Hiding underneath the mattress
When she finds them
There is a fire in the backyard
A surprise
To mark the occasion
Nothing is said
But he knows what is burning there
God and Mother
Joined together
A holy inferno
For the dirty magazines
Retribution
For a bedroom secret
Badly hid

'Little boys who read these magazines grow up to be rapists.'
So his Mother says

Naked ladies and demons
Caught in the cross fire
Of God's gun
Every bullet is an ejaculation
Every prayer
A spiritual parole
Another weeping hole
In God's wayward son

Masturbating
On his way to eternity
On his back
On his knees
Time to pray
He'll be the first Australian Pope
So his Mother says
One day

If Only

If I were a Carpenter
I would nail you to an angry cross
I would build a church
Out of your despair

If I were a Magician
I would make you disappear
And then search for you in vain

If I were a Sculptor
I would carve you
Into someone more hateable
Host an exhibition
Of all the versions of you
That I love and loathe
A put-on display for tart lovers
And high society reptiles

If I were a Firefighter
I would set you alight
Over and over again
Just so I could put out the purple fires
Dancing in the cavernous holes
Where your eyes used to be

If I were a Chef
I would serve up your flesh
To a restaurant of affluent cannibals

If I were a Comedian
I would make you laugh so hard
You would wet yourself
I would retract all of the obvious punchlines
I would punch myself in the face

If I were a Banker
I would save up just to purchase you
Then bury you in blood money

If I were a Doctor
I would prescribe you personality pills
I would bulk bill your enemies
And tell you, smiling all the while
That you only have one week to live

If I were a Sailor
I would sink your ship
I would toss you punctured floaties
Cast an inflatable lifeline
Into your deflated, raging sea

If I were a Musician
I would serenade you with strings and wings
And lightly pluck your harpy heart

If I were an Astronaut
I would space the fuck out
And ask you to marry me on the moon

If I were a Tree
I would be all about the autumn leavings
And I would surely leave you
For someone with a chainsaw
And a wandering eye for taller trees

If I were a Film-maker
I would immortalise you digitally
Then direct your directionless act

If I were a Computer
I would save you and then delete you
I would cut you
Copy and paste your viral face

If I were a Serial Killer
I would confess all of my kills to you
I would even let you sniff the corpses
I would promise not to murder your enthusiasm
Or bury you alive

If I were a Writer
I would address my suicide note
To you…

Caught Jester

Am I your Jester?
No one else shall wipe the smut from this picture
Am I your Cancer?
No one else shall wipe the grin from this sphincter
Am I your Spider?
The fangs in your punctured umbrella
When it's pouring rain…

A life sentence without punctuation
Just pills with unpronounceable names
A naked, cracked egg-hell
This cosmic joke, this prison yoke, scrambled
Without the possibility of parole

Am I your Jester?
The lie in the web, the fractured mirror
The self-sanctioned director
Are my jokes getting better?
The smear of the tears
And the sickness, the hopelessness
The only certainty, the calamity
Serving deserving royal tea
A song and dance frown clown
Holding court in low places
Bowing to the unclean Queen
With slip slop slapstick pomposity
Caught Jestering again

Suicide, this creeping compunction
My daydreaming damnation
The daddy of the dragons
Plot hatched in a Game of Groans
The crippled contagion
No forgiveness, just pale contrition
Lost at sea in a mutiny of semen
With no way back to the shore

When you left me here
I cried myself a curious river
But the past life preserver
Kept me relevant, buoyant, free
Now I'm paddling in circles
For the Reality Tourists
An Entertainer, burnt beetroot red
Bummed by the Unchosen Son

Am I your Jester?
A burping heart, pumping cruel fiction
Obliterated by yet another callous edit
Misread, unsaid, all of it
The whole in my head
Host to a carnival graveyard
Dotted with Wombstones
Shrouded in clitoral pink fog
A first and last eulogy
For the ultimate fool

It is the Unknowing Certainty of it all
This is the First page of The End

Pork Crackling is the Devil

the devil is pork crackling
the devil is the best and worst fuck you ever had
the devil is a Cuban cigar and a Marxist subtext
the devil is love and death by sexuality
the devil is instant pasta karma without the bitch
the devil is gourmet coffee and that morning after bitterness
the devil is the last course of action in a one course death row meal
the devil is a drug without consequences
the devil is forgiveness in a whiskey bottle
the devil is pornographic redemption
the devil is a feminist torpedoing through a glass sky

the devil is your best friend when you have no one
the devil is a nuclear bomb gathering cobwebs and dust
the devil is masturbation sans the guilt
the devil is soul food and a planet of cheese
the devil is an orbiting medication moon
the devil is the driver in peak hour traffic who lets you in
the devil is bacon and circumcision enduring a Judaic orgy
the devil is everyday madness and imaginative suicide
the devil is the potential of a held sledgehammer surrounded by walls
the devil is a homeless Santa and a good father
the devil is a mother who loves you despite it all

god is a smug motherfucker
god is a bad priest
god is road rage and a mobile phone
god is the drunken prick who kicked you over and over until you pissed blood
god is incest and long jail paragraphs and short sentences
god is war and unreasonable violence
god is a Hollywood blockbuster starring artificially sweetened superheroes
god is a sociopath with soft wandering hands and big plans
god is the official bus driver for human trafficking
god is a malignant narcissist
god is an American president

god is a gang of angry teenagers on meth
god is your brain on ice
god is a racist bigot who attempts to argue with logic
god is domestic violence and emotional terrorism served with a side salad of hell
god is a billboard advertisement for sexual harassment
god is an important promise repeatedly broken
god is an unrepentant bully

god is just another reason to hate yourself,
the whole fucking world and everything in it

the devil is the reason you are still smiling

Dark Matters

The Enemy told me:

All that you know, see and feel
Is wrong

Several automated monkeys
Leapt from the screen
And proclaimed me King
I asked them rhetorical questions
They gathered around me
Garnishing my crown
With meaningful silences
Saying nothing and everything
All at once
In reverent tones

The Enemy told me:

All you are is flesh and cheese
No moral can contain you
Your anguish is cheddar
Several automated versions of me
Leapt back through the screen
Curious, wondering
What is this strange land
That the monkeys call a home?

The Enemy told me:

You will find yourself there
And you will never be able to leave

The Enemy warned me:

Prisons such as these are custom built
They contain no one but you
All of the mirrors
Will reflect only you
All of the jailers
Will look exactly like you
And they will treat you
As you have treated yourself

I shuddered,
I closed my eyes and I ran
And the weight of a mad world
Collapsing
Bore down upon me
Cement tears turned to concrete
And set hard upon my cheeks

Then all the filth and horror
The disgust and loathing
All the blah, blah, fucking blah,
Terror, guilt, hate and sorrow
Formed into three
        simple
        words

And the Enemy waved goodbye, whispering:

I love you.

Gimcrack

Welcome to Emosexuality
In this kissable
Foaming-at-the-mouth-pharmacy
The shelves are shaking all around me
Closing in, raining down
Like scattered needles
Thrown needlessly into the air

Two papier mâché approximations
Of an angel and an astronaut
Fight over a manuscript on madness
And a reason to call the moon their own

I am rattling with the chattering
Of plastic wind-up teeth
An exploding puffer fish
A rubber hand grenade
With a pullable pun
A ceramic schizophrenic
With a fragile smile

The cameras roll like bones
Should I smile and wave?
The particle accelerator
Causes me to crumble like chunks of dry
Misbegotten wedding cake
All over this marriage
Of horror and broken plastic figurines

You and I
No longer dancing to 80s classics
On the third tier tower of icing
And sweet snow frosting
All over the inevitable divorce
Between loneliness and shelf space
Between the deepest holes
In grinding gear teeth
And the unstoppable oozing
Of tarmacadam toothpaste

Poisoned melancholic drifters
Just waiting to out-wait death
It's raining pills
Taxi's spontaneously combust
Breaking into laughter
As the pebbles of psychotropic ponce
Serenade us with Cupid's final bow

A pickled eyeball in a murky jar
Sinking, unblinking
Searching the mind for secrets
Don't trip on the stares
Don't forget to be home
Before the stroke of midnight
Soon all of this will disappear
The music will stop
The lights will fade
The flesh will fall from my bones

The dance is over, still
The smiling of strangers lingers
The retarded joy
Swept away by a styrofoam janitor
Who should have known better

Plastic Gandhi is dead
Claymation Allah caught a leaking ferry
To the other side
Wooden Elvis split while the going was bad
Lego Jesus was decapitated
Lost his head
Just another fallen mirror ball
Caved in, cracked and seceded from the fall
Lolling like a damaged loon
In a neon pool of tears

The Giant and the Boy 2

The Giant sits the Boy in front of the mirror
and cuts his hair.
The Boy sits as still as he can.
The Giant squints his eyes,
red with the drink,
and hacks off big chunks of the Boy's hair.

The Boy left the scissors at school.
So to teach him a lesson
the Giant cuts his hair
with an old-fashioned shaving razor.

The Boy wets himself.
Hot piss trickles down his legs
and onto the hair on the floor.
The Giant's face twists into disgust.
He cannot look at the Boy.
Before he leaves,
he tells the Boy to clean himself up
and go to bed.

The Boy knows it is the Maggot's fault, not his.
He sits there, glaring at the Maggot in the mirror.
Just like the Giant glares at him.

'You disgust me,' he says.

The next morning the Giant sends the Boy to school.
The Boy sits staring at the teacher
standing in front of the blackboard.
He is aware of the other boys seated behind him.
Whispering and giggling
whenever the teacher turns away.

The Boy knows they are making fun of him.
Little missiles of warm spittle and paper
sting the back of his neck.
One slides under his collar and he feels it
slowly trickle down his spine

One side of his scalp is clipped short
and the other is long and uncut.
The teacher turns away,
and the missiles hiss past his ears
and stick in what is left of his hair.

After class, the Boy deliberately pisses himself again.
He hopes that if he stinks of piss,
They will leave him alone.

A Public Display of Infection

1.

your mouth is an open wound
my fist plunges deep inside of you
and I pull back a bloody stump

there must be an easier way to
tear out your heart I've tried
everything except loving you

I don't understand you I
underestimate your every move
this is like playing chess in blood

if I knew how to imitate your
particular brand of chaos we could
get married and fuck at other people's

funerals like it doesn't matter…it
never mattered My Dear not even the
open displays of public infection that

entertained even the disaffected, those
well-meaning jackals who jack off and
hammer their blitzing bits like jizz nails

into stained glass vials that were meant
for tears like ours…oh My Dear what a
wasted opportunity to serve you up as
the main course of this gala I call entropy

I guess I should have rolled you out
of the oven while you still had
plump red lips with which to kiss me

2.

life is a long, meandering reptile,
a grinning game show host, a bumbling joke,
dressed in a pink sequinned tuxedo,
waving maniacally at passing ambulances and
cock cars with sirens squealing
like stuck pigs in slow-motion quicksand

dying is the part that sucks the
marrow from your bones and defames
you My Dear…it's the part that hurts the most
just close your eyes and try to force a smile
it will all be over soon enough

death is an unfortunate punchline
it means nothing to very little at all
but if executed correctly
it
can
be
absolutely
fucking
hilarious.

Waiting in the Endless Queue for the Afterlife

This is a waiting game
This is a waiting room
This is your waiting cream
Apply it thoroughly and thoughtfully
To your nether regions
Your arm pits, face, skin and hair
Lather your mind, heart and soul
In electric Elvis mayonnaise
And jailhouse rock 'n' roll

This is your love lotion
This is your love notion
It will render you
Infinitely desirable
Although, we have no way to know
Whether that is true
Product testing is expensive and
There is so much else we'd rather do

TickTock
TickTock

Welcome to the official Mass Debate
This distant planetary mind prison
Tis a ceremony stretched across dimensions
For maudlin debaters en masse

Calculate the exact trajectory
Of your closing argument carefully
And by all means
Do breathe in the deleterious air

You are in a long, long queue
There are millions upon billions
Waiting in line ahead of you

TickTock
TickTock

We will get to you eventually
Even if it takes an eternity
So guzzle the complimentary Kool Aid
Ready your mind
Sharpen your weapon
Thank your corporate sponsors
Gamble with death responsibly and quietly and
Ponder the untold wonders of heaven

There is an invisible crucifix
Trained between your eyes
The Angels have you in their cross hairs
So no sudden movements, please…
Take a seat
We will deal with you shortly
Seraphim are renowned
For their itchy trigger fingers and
God is hungry
For monkey meat

(Bang?)

No, best to remain moonshine still
Cower, drunken in the spotlight
Mentally recite your confessions
Your saintly axe
Your past life transgressions

We are all watching.
We are all being watched.
Waiting.
Dying.
Reading.
Writing.
Being read as we are written.
Written off as read.
Dead?

TickTock
TickTock

Rest assured
Your prayers will be answered in due course
It's just a matter of time
Time
Time
Time
Time
Time
Time
Time…

End of Level Boss

End of Level Boss
Towering above me
My poems are grenades
My words are shotgun shells
My imagination is a weapon
I strafe
I shoot
I pull puns and seduce nuns
I lob poems at poets like Eden's apples
And the shame shimmers

End of Level Boss
Languishing on a thoughtless throne
My pages are toilet paper
Inked like stink
Illuminating brown rainbows
My mind is a wet sock
Sulking in a vast porcelain ocean
The ammunition floats just beneath the surface
My tears are bullets wept

End of Level Boss
Glowing in the gutter
Outshining Orion's belt of stars
Feeding personality pellets
To the scene machines
To dilettantes and shooting scars
I waver, like bad body odour
Impotent deodorant
Poking holes in ozone

Saving up
For that hipster replacement operation
No more limping away from the in-crowd
A leprous literary insect
Unheard and unseen

End of Level Boss
Looming above me
Genius in the devilled egg detail
Another cracking yawn
Another grass-is-greener lawn
Another cultural attaché to the king within

End of Level Boss
Another God of Poetry
Gathering the gifted to her breast
As they suckle on her spotlit tit
Waxing lyrical like Icarus
Melting on sunnily disposed stages
Meant for delusional saviours

End of Level Boss
Filling the skies with the milk of his eyes
Choking my insecurities
Captured like a drunk gnat
In his pixellated fist

End of Level Boss
Ricocheting off the scribblings in my head
Swaying like a medicated hammock
In a dyslexic word asylum
Painting the padded walls with Manson's shit

End of Level Boss
Indebted
To the bursting bladders of word giants
And the bowel Howl
Of Ginsberg's echoed Moloch
And Bukowski's swaggering grace

End of Level Boss
The imaginary monster
The writer, unread
Falling like Pharisees
Toppled like Crooked-Timber trees
Shot
Point-blank
Dead

When He Wrote About the Events That Led To This

He was the kind of man who called a spade a trowel
He dug for diamonds in shit
Deep, deep his reach
Deep, deep his mind swam
Into the foul wretch of his yesterdays

He smelt of bleached plastic roses and arsenic
Forever running up endless, poisoned hills
Sweating his way into an advertised heaven
Where pigs were finally men
And little boys dreamt of billboards
Big enough to block out the Son

When he wrote about the events that led to this
He was ahead of the curve
And the roads wound around his pricked fingers
Like shrivelled old Band-Aids
That had long lost the will to stick to wounds

When it was time for him to write
He was already halfway home
Panicked ambulances chased him
Their sirens squealing like swine
Women with nothing better to do swooned
Snipers held him in their cross hairs
Tempted by itchy trigger fingers
And the unseemly bobble of his bulbous head

When he wrote about the events that led to this
He thought fondly of the disco cancers
That riddled his dance floor liver
He inhaled unrequited love
As the smoke machine of death
Pissed rogue smog into his nightclub lungs

When he wrote about the events that led to this
The point itself became pointless
The words crawled into his eyes, ears and nose
Like pregnant insects
With gutloads of eggs to blow
All over the plump Christmas turkey
Roasted, bloated and basted
Glistening and soon wasted
Due to the lone literary fly
Shitting wordplay like larvae
Ruining the feast for the entire family
Who moments before the explosion
Had lowered their heads in solemn prayer

'God bless this mess!' they wept.

Blasts of violent projectile vomit
Shot across the dining room table
The feast caught in the crossfire
The unholy ooze, lathering the gathering
Exploding
In the stretched to snapping
Festive faces
Of a family well done

The Boxer

When I was a fighter
I had no father in my corner
I wept concrete tears after every loss
I got knocked on my arse a thousand times
Lost every bout, won every toss

When I was a fighter
I drank a bathtub of my own blood
I ate nails and shit
Knuckle bones and teeth
I kissed the girls and killed my friends
Never made a mistake I didn't mean
Never made amends

When I was a fighter
God bet against me
I fought the world upon an altar
I mainlined the holy water
I sacked my coach and turned to booze

When I was a fighter
I was told I couldn't win
The audience cheered for someone else
Every punch I took was comic gold
Every nightmare I had was therapy
A title fight
At twenty-one years old

When I was a fighter
I just stood there and absorbed every blow
I performed my lowly eulogy
I learned I am the enemy
I danced with Diablo, ate his halo
Snorted the piss-yellow cocaine snow

When I lost my mind
I grinned for the cameras
Like a leprous loon
Speed dialled a metaphysical pizza
Booty called Mother Teresa
Told her I'd be home soon

When I lost my way
I ended up here
Punching keys instead of faces
On a midnight stage of pages
The fight is over
You gave no quarter
The fight is over
I am done

The Words Have Turned Their Backs On Us

I cannot write, he wrote.

Nobody smiles around here any more
The laughter is long gone
The words have turned their backs on us
We look forward to the past
We worship in the red-light district
Catch clapping
Like a leprous prostitute
In an ad for phantom limbs

I have nothing to say, he said.

On blustery moors
Our bones chill and sink
The wind has teeth
We are up to our necks in mud jazz
Mute trumpet blasts echo
Across wet canyon landfill
The concrete is setting
Like cold grey Sundays
In churches made of turning meat

I cannot cry, he cried.

We were of fire
Now we are extinguished
Wallowing in a flatulent dawn
Stinking of nonsense and prayer and regret

We were of passion
Now we are victims of reality
Dull-fuckings
Gripped by the red-handed fists
Of murderers and dead kings

We were of art
Now we are copies of copies of copies
Released in a limited run
Of stammering centre stages

So I cannot ask questions? He asked.

No, I am not replying to that, She replied.

And the poem ended…
And not a moment too soon
Like a crescent moon leapt by villainous shadows
It was over.

Unborn Again

I am the swamp divinity built
I am guilt
Do you need to drag the waters?
What are you looking for?
Beautiful, Hollywood corpses
With dead, unblinking eyes
And smiling Botox faces?

The International Necrophilia Convention
Rises to their feet
And rigidly applauds you
You deserve their undying love
A standing ovulation

Have I angered your God?
Does she even give a fuck?

Don't kid yourself, the Voice says.

Debauched thoughts
Pile on top of me like angry lemmings
Diseased, aroused, oozing black light
Gnawing on my forgetful bones

Disgust surges through my veins
Like dishwashing detergent pestilence
Home brand
Third aisle on the left
A red-light district special
For churchgoers with unspecial needs
And the regulated consciences
Of uppity God schmoozers

Take a seat, kneel, stand, kneel again and repeat after me,
The Voice says.

One cannot dream in such conditions
The pain in my knees wards off the snoring

Still, I am drugged by the Word
Pummelled by another tedious Sunday sermon
Delivered with unconvincing panache
By a sweaty priest with a moist secret
Proselytising to undercover Satanists
From behind his morally ambiguous pulpit

Yes, boredom can kill you, the Voice says… And it will.

There are spiders in my blood
There are wasted, drug-fucked ghosts
Vomiting on the other side of the curtain
Paranormal puke defines me
Like pornographic gunk
And frisky dolphin spunk
It collects like miracles
In the corners of my dream-deprived eyes

Don't fucking move! the Voice says.

I dare not
Lest I be eaten alive
By pretty, death-wish butterflies
Fluttering in and out of formation

Still, this tomb is an open womb
And I am unborn again
and again
and again

You mean less than nothing, the Voice says.

And so it is Unwritten
And so we are Unborn
The imaginatively mortal mistake
That thinking monkeys make
Is believing that they actually matter

Balmy Rubble

Trapped here
Under layers of rubble
I wonder about those above me
Digging for animated flesh
And flailing consciousness

In all this mess of death
And a trillion brain bells
Slain, ringing
From a phone booth
On the other side of the wall
For someone to save them
For someone to save me
From myself

But the ringing won't stop
And no one answers that phone
And those digging for life
I somehow know
Will one day give up
And leave those of us
Unmoving
Barely breathing
Still alive under all this debris
To fend for ourselves

Jesus: A Version

The Boy, centre cage
Hiding in the back row
Of a Christian choir hell
He sings
But no sound comes out
He screams
But no-one hears him

The Boy, home alone
He blubbers incoherently
Presses his face into the screen
He gnashes his television teeth
The white noise, inaudible
Beneath the raw cacophony
Of the other animals on display
Hungry
Slavering
Pacing all around him
Drawing ever closer

Sometimes
When a mind is truly broken
There is no recourse
But deviant reaction
No conveniently inconvenient exit
No fucking redemption

All of these turpitudes
They equal a life
Of teething, baby death steps
One by one by one
They tear at themselves
Echoes of echoes of boot heels
Clapping upon a path
Few dare tread

What coffin do they seek?
Blood shadows hissing
Oozing life lost
Who would hold this box of ending?
The bearers
They march towards a hole
That cannot contain such demons

A plague of poetry
A fictional reality
Gnawed angle grinder fingernails
Spraying the sky like wood chips
From sullen, buzzing lumber yards
The swirling of misery's leaves
The crackling of brittle, bush fire incisors
Swallowed like communion

The mind's harvest, unfathomable
A lonely puppet
Dangling in perfumed vomit
Rivers of cheap piss
Choking the seepage
In fields that go on forever
Beyond the reach of sanity
Clogging life's steady drain

Jesus wept?

You bet…
He bawled his fucking eyes out.

The Giant and the Boy 3

Tied to a tree in the backyard
and not allowed to come back inside.
Is this a dream, the Boy wonders?
Through his eyes there is a mirror
suspended from the branch of the tree.
The Giant who lives in the house put it there,
To teach the Boy something.

'You are a Maggot, a pathetic Maggot,' the Giant says,
'And that is all you will ever be!'

'See…' the Giant says, 'there!'
He points at the little Maggot in the mirror
with his giant finger.

The Boy does not know what a Maggot is,
but he knows it is ugly and it is in the mirror.
He can't help looking at it,
at the Maggot in the mirror,
tied to a big tree so it can hardly move.

Night falls and the boy watches in awe
as a creeping fog engulfs the moon.
Soon he can barely see the Maggot
and the wind whips the mirror from side to side.
There is a rumble and an explosion of light.
The Mouth in the Sky cackles with laughter.
The roar of heavy rain envelopes the darkness.
The storm cleanses the Boy's wounds,
soothing his parched throat.

When the storm passes,
and the light of the moon spills across the yard,
the little Boy realises
that the mirror and the branch are gone.

Dozens of glass shards
are scattered across the grass,
each catching the light of the moon
like a star.

The branch that held the mirror
has fallen and landed at the Boy's feet.
Torn from the tree like the arm of the Giant…
Defeated by the storm.

www.ingramcontent.com/pod-product-compliance
Lightning Source LLC
Chambersburg PA
CBHW070919080526
44589CB00013B/1372